NATIONAL GEOGRAPHIC

School Publishing

Keeping Fit

Zeina Mahran

PICTURE CREDITS

Illustration by Ivan Finnegan (14–15).

Cover, 1, 2, 4 (all), 5 (above right), 6, 7 (left), 8, 9 (all), 10 (right), 11 (below), 13 (all), 14 (center), 15 (center & below), Photolibrary.com; 5 (left), 7 (right), 10 (left), 11 (above right), 12, 15 (above), Getty Images; 5 (below right), 14 (above & below), APL/Corbis.

Produced through the worldwide resources of the National Geographic Society, John M. Fahey, Jr., President and Chief Executive Officer; Gilbert M. Grosvenor, Chairman of the Board; Nina D. Hoffman, Executive Vice President and President, Books and Education Publishing Group.

PREPARED BY NATIONAL GEOGRAPHIC SCHOOL PUBLISHING

Ericka Markman, Senior Vice President and President Children's Books and Education Publishing Group; Steve Mico, Senior Vice President and Publisher; Marianne Hiland, Editorial Director; Lynnette Brent, Executive Editor; Michael Murphy and Barbara Wood, Senior Editors; Bea Jackson, Design Director; David Dumo, Art Director; Margaret Sidlowsky, Illustrations Director; Matt Wascavage, Manager of Publishing Services; Sean Philpotts, Production Manager.

MANUFACTURING AND QUALITY MANAGEMENT

Christopher A. Liedel, Chief Financial Officer; Phillip L. Schlosser, Director; Clifton M. Brown III, Manager.

BOOK DEVELOPMENT

Ibis for Kids Australia Pty Limited.

Published by the National Geographic Society
1145 17th Street, N.W.
Washington, D.C. 20036-4688

ISBN-13: 978-0-7922-6069-1
ISBN-10: 0-7922-6069-4

6 7 19 18
Printed in USA

Contents

walk

swim

run

play

ride a bike

5

Fit and Healthy

Exercise helps you keep fit and healthy. There are many ways to exercise.

play basketball

swim

skate

7

Fun and Games

There are fun ways to exercise.
You exercise when you play active games.

jump rope

play hopscotch

play soccer

Everyday Activities

You can exercise when you do everyday activities.

sweep

wash a car

climb stairs

walk a dog

11

Energy for Exercise

You need energy to exercise.
Eating healthy food gives you energy.

Sleep gives you energy, too.

Green Park

exercise

fun

game

healthy

keep fit

park

play

run

walk

Picture Glossary

basketball

eat

hopscotch

play

skate

sleep

soccer

swim